European History: The Most Important Leaders, Events, & People Through "European History" That Shaped Europe and Eventually Became the: European Union

information contained within this document, including, but not limited to, —errors, omissions, or inaccuracies.

Table of Contents

Introduction

PROBABLY THE BEST BOOK CLUB ONLINE...

"If you love books. You will <u>love</u> the Lean Stone Book Club"

*** <u>Exclusive Deals</u> That <u>Any</u> Book Fan Would <u>Love!</u> ***

Visit leanstonebookclub.com/join

to find out more

(IT'S FREE)!

The **History of Europe** was shaped by numerous events, of political, social and cultural nature, and by the input of influential personalities, such as **Johannes Gutenberg, Martin Luther, The Sun King,** Napoleon Bonaparte, Queen Victoria, and so on. Change and development happened slowly, yet steadily, and each factor played a significant role in the development of Europe, events which, after centuries, have contributed to the establishment of the **European Union.**

In the Middle Ages, the society was centered on the concepts and theology promoted by the Church, which was recognized as the Supreme Authority. Notwithstanding, the growing interest in ancient Greek and Roman art, together with the scholars' orientation towards *the man,* as opposed to *God – the divinity,* marked the beginning of Renaissance – a time when Europe experienced a rebirth. The involvement of Protestant reformers, such as Martin Luther, Jean Calvin, and others, established a new dimension to the way in which the Church should be considered. And this was another step Europe took towards development.

A time of industrialization and revolution followed, which enhanced the power and wealth for the class of entrepreneurs and manufacturers. This period was marked by the French Revolution, which was followed by other movements of the same nature. From that point, the European society was headed towards establishing a new class, which would become dominant – the working class. In that scenario, the government had to be reformed, as the focus wasn't placed on attending the needs of the greater majority of people. This facilitated the forging of new, modern ideologies, including liberalism, capitalism, and communism, which constructed the grounds of today's democratic Europe.

The elements enumerated above constitute only a brief introduction into the fascinating European realm. This book aims at presenting the main events that formed the **European History** and triggered its continual evolution. Therefore, without further ado, let's delve into this abundant, compelling historical territory, and find answers to your most intriguing questions!

Chapter 1 - The Renaissance – The *Rebirth* of Europe

There are numerous personalities and leaders who have played a crucial part in the development of Europe, as we know it today. It is implied that the European Union is the outcome of the implications of prominent individualities, who have made progress possible through advancement and by embracing change. We will track down the dominant events that facilitated the development of the European population, from a political point of view, and from a cultural mindset as well.

To begin with, the Renaissance is recognized as a movement of cultural and scholar nature, which accentuated the rediscovery of texts originating from classic antiquity. It's important to grasp that the Renaissance did not occur all of a sudden, but it was determined by an enumeration of events, which further triggered the facts that constituted the Renaissance.

In essence, this movement originated in Italy, at the initiative of Petrarch, who was devotedly passionate about rediscovering ancient manuscripts. In other words, the movement was oriented towards comprehending the ancient knowledge from the ancient Roman and Greek eras. Renaissance is translated into *rebirth,* as previously stated. The question is, what role did this cultural movement that took place during the 1400 – 1600 play in altering **European History?**

You see, everything that occurred throughout history contributed to the way in which things are, at the time being. And Renaissance was a campaign featured by dynamism, as European discoverers were eager to explore new terrains and unknown continents. Concurrently, the trading methods and patterns suffered consistent changes, and a considerable amount of scientific discoveries were noted. We could affirm that most of these scientific discoveries were, to some extent, triggered by the movement. For instance, that of the printing press, which is, until today, acknowledged as an innovation of majestic significance.

Why was the Renaissance different?

Classical culture experienced a range of *rebirths* during this time. But the primary aspect that featured this movement was that this revival was triggered by numerous elements including cultural, scholarly, and political ones. During this time, the old structures of political and social nature were replaced with new concepts and beliefs. In other words, a new elite was materialized, and it was featured by innovative ideas and patterns of thinking.

As the Renaissance period evolved, the Italian cities from which the movement originally sprung competed with one another for attaining wealth and boosting civic pride. In essence, they were autonomous, and due to the Mediterranean trade routes, the number of merchants and artisans was significantly high.

At the top hierarchy of the Italian society, there were these *new men,* whose positions were confirmed by their renowned wealth and power, which they were keen on demonstrating.

The Renaissance – liberty and learning

An increased interest in republicanism and liberty was noted. Furthermore, there was a significant change in the attitude towards pre-Christian books, as previously outlined. Thus, the classical ideas and mindsets began to influence people. Without fear of contradiction, one of the most significant changes was the foundation of public libraries, which facilitated the spread of information, and a growing interest in studying was noted. The introduction of the printing press lead to an explosion of texts, and also contributed to establishing the foundation of the modern world.

Johannes Gutenberg – the man behind the world's greatest inventions

During the Renaissance, one invention became of crucial importance, which made it possible for medieval Europe to embrace modern thinking. I'm referring, of course, to the printing press. Before the creation of the printing press, books were scarce, and information wasn't at everyone's disposal. In this context, the press instituted the modern age of literacy and initiated the process of making knowledge available to the common man.

Back in 868 CE, in China, the existence of printed books was noted. Still, the system had its limitations. Some of the papers which were previously block printed – the words were carved into blocks made of wood, which were afterward rolled with ink, and imprinted into the paper. Europeans embraced this technique, but it was costly and took a lot of time. Johannes **Gutenberg** was the European that fulfilled the demand for a better, more efficient printing system.

Johannes Gutenberg was born in the south of Germany, and his date of birth is assumed to be on June 24th, 1400. He wasn't rich, nor did he possess a high rank in society, and worked as a gem cutter and goldsmith. His invention was revolutionary and innovative; this is an event that cannot be paralleled with any other device on European ground.

He replaced the wood, which was tough to work with, and decided to work with metal instead. He was inspired by rural wine making in creating the machine; the system was simple to use, and would finally facilitate the expansion of information, making education more accessible. The first book he printed was the Bible, as it was expected of that time.

Gutenberg wanted to keep his invention a secret and exploit his discovery. Unfortunately, that wasn't possible, since the idea was soon spread in the most important European cities by 1500. Finally, this invention facilitated the availability of information through readable material, with diminished costs. Concurrently, Renaissance meant more opportunities for people to study and obtain an education, which was made possible only with the innovative creation of the printing press.

Experts and scholars would finally have the possibility to study texts, without fearing that the scribe might have slipped an error or two. The modern exchange of knowledge, whether it's done on through printed word, or on the internet has commenced with the innovative invention of this one man, who has facilitated the establishment of the modern world as we know it today.

The Black Death

The **Black Death** also referred to as *The Plague*, or the *Great Mortality* is acknowledged as an Epidemic, which took place during 1346 – 1353. The plague erased one-third of the world population, being officially recognized as the most severe natural disaster in history. Concurrently, this epidemic has altered the course of history. The question that typically arises is why? Let's see how these aspects are interconnected.

The infection was spread by fleas, which were infected by a bacterium known as *Yersinia Pestis*. The bacterium dwelled on rats that lived on ships, in particular, and among men. After being infected, the animal died, and the fleas would further affect the humans. The starting point of the Black Death was on the northwest shores of the Caspian Sea, and it spread to Europe when an Italian trading post in Crimea suffered a Mongolian attack.

The plague traveled rapidly, affecting the European population, particularly the thriving European ports. During the cold weather, the rapidity of the plague was slowed down, but the disease wasn't eradicated. In 1353, when the plague arrived on Russian land, only a few countries have been spared – Iceland and Finland, as they didn't play a significant role in international trade.

At that time, the people assumed that the plague was sent by God, in order to punish them for their sins. The medical knowledge was restricted, which prevented the development of efficient treatments. There were some assumptions that improper hygiene was somehow linked to the plague, and the King of England took the initiative of cleaning up the streets. Nonetheless, the root of the problem – the fleas and rats, wasn't addressed.

Although the plague ended in 1353, Europe was tormented with the infection for centuries. Few hundred years later, in the seventeenth century, thanks to medical advancements, the disease consistently decreased, until it was eradicated on European land.

Consequences of the Black Death

The immediate outcome of the Black Death was an unexpected downfall in trade, and an interruption of military conflicts. Nonetheless, as soon as the spread of the infection was stopped, these were soon re-established. Other effects, of a long-term nature, include the diminishing of cultivated land,

and an increase in labor costs. Due to the shortage of working population, this enabled the working class to ask increased compensation for their work. The same principle applied to skilled professionals. These changes, together with the increased social mobility have featured the Renaissance period. Concurrently, as the number of people who were wealthy was significantly lower, there were more funds to be allocated to religious and cultural objects of value.

On the other hand, the position of the landowners was undermined, as hiring labor force was costly; this encouraged the development of cost-effective, modern devices. We could say that, from multiple points of view, the Black Death facilitated the transfer from the medieval era, to the modern era. The Renaissance movement has altered the way in which people conveyed life, and this is imminently linked to the horrific plague.

In northern Europe, the plague affected the evolution of art, as the artistic movement aimed at portraying death, and what happens afterward, in numerous cultures and religions. The strength of the church was diminished, as people would search for answers – why did the plague exterminate one-third of the world's population?

Check your understanding!

1. What are the primary aspects that facilitated the Renaissance? Which are the fundamental ideas and concepts that differentiated this period from the Middle Ages?
2. In what way did the Black Death ensure development in the European framework? How did it impact the position of the working class?

3. Highlight the importance of the printing press in Europe. How is the invention of the printing press related to the Renaissance movement and the road towards modernity?

Chapter 2 - The Reformation and Its Imminent Consequences

The Reformation is recognized as the rupture from the Latin Christian church, which was prompted by **Martin Luther**, in 1517. This movement determined the development of other similar campaigns which are known, until today, as Protestantism.

The establishment of a new Christian faith has opened the road towards freedom of thought. The context in which the reformation took place is a complex one. In the early 16th century, the Latin Church was ruled by one single figure – the Pope, who had significant power in the affairs of the state as well.

In other words, religion infiltrated every single aspect of the society – the poor were religious as they wanted to have the reassurance of a better afterlife. They were afflicted, and their lives were hard and arduous. Still, the church didn't provide them satisfaction nor consolation, as it was driven by an arrogant mindset, avarice, it abused power, and was featured by pompous bureaucracy. The discrepancy between the way in which the churches were constructed, and people's homes and livelihood was bombastic.

Reformation was expected

There was a unanimous agreement according to which the church needed restoration, to be re-initiated to its pure form. Nevertheless, the church was resistant to change; the attempts for reformation were inconsistent. The main aspect that blocked change was the belief that the church alone provided the path to salvation. Thus, there was an urgent need for proof, which would demonstrate that the people don't need the Catholic Church in order to obtain salvation and redemption from their sins. And Martin Luther was up for the challenge.

In 1517, Martin Luther – theology professor, presented 95 theses against the selling of indulgences. What were these indulgences? These indulgences were sold by the Catholic Church to fellow Christian men; and, in return, they would be provided atonement for their sins and transgressions. In his theses, Luther attacked the matter of indulgences. He actually nailed the list of arguments on the door of the church, and the rupture was made.

The pope condemned Luther, but he supported his theses with the Scripture and challenged the papal authority and the origins of the Catholic Church. Luther's style in preaching attracted a wide number of people – he determined other preachers among Germany to embrace his ideas. It was the first time when a new way of thinking like that would be embraced by the public in such a short amount of time. The people yearned for reformation, and it was given to them.

Luther outlined that, salvation was made possible with faith in God, and he highlighted the importance of the Scripture, which should have been made available to the poor as well. Additionally, he didn't agree with the pompous hierarchy that was typical to the Catholic Church. Instead, he wanted the church to have a more simple structure. In essence, the costly, grandiose, elaborate and organized church with uncaring priests was replaced by Protestantism, where teaching, praying and worshipping were of central focus for the believers.

In spite of the opposing actions of church governments, and, of course, the Pope, Protestantism has established itself permanently in Europe. The consequences were notable, changing people's mindset on faith and religion. Historians argue that, among the personal reasons why people embraced Protestantism, and the belief in the new message, there was the possibility of seizing land from the church, while relishing freedom from the restrictions imposed by the church.

The Reformation made the Bible available to the masses, which the Catholic Church didn't encourage. Because of this event, the New World received its form, as the number of missionaries throughout the globe increased. The Reformation liberated the people from restrictions and granted them freedom of thought and action. In many ways, the movement has simplified things, by diminishing the influence of the Catholic Church.

Check your understanding!

1. How did the people convey the religious authority, namely the Pope, and how is it related to the imminence of the Reformation?
2. In what way was the occurrence of the Reformation foretold by Renaissance thinking?
3. How did the Reformation facilitate the road towards modernity?

Chapter 3 - Prominent Representatives of the Monarchy in Europe

The Sun King – Louis XIV

There are some dominant personalities that leave their mark in history – one of them is Louis XIV, also referred to as **The Sun King**. He was a French monarch, who started his reign in 1642, and ruled until 1715. The success of his absolutist reign granted him the title of *the Sun King*.

In 1661, Louis XIV began reforming France, as, until that moment, Chief Minister Cardinal Jules Mazarin prevented him from exercising his power. Even though his mother – Anne of Austria had the position of regent, the most influential figure at that time was Mazarin.

He wanted to reform France, in lines with his personal vision. In 1661, Louis affirmed that he wanted to rule without the assistance of a chief minister. He considered himself to be the representative of God on earth; therefore, he assumed that he was offered total power and control over the country. Thereupon, his emblem, as the Sun King further illustrates his acclaimed omnipotence.

The focus is directed towards industrialization and development

His initial purpose was to promote industrial growth, by establishing reforms. Additionally, he wanted to assume absolute control of France and the colonies overseas. In this direction, Jean-Baptiste Colbert, in the position of the finance minister introduced a series of reforms, which stimulated the economic growth of the country.

Concurrently, war minister Marquis de Louvois focused on expanding and modernizing the French army. At the same time, he managed to ameliorate the situation of the rebellious nobles, who have aroused 11 civil wars in four decades, by attracting them to the court with the luxurious lifestyle. In this direction, he built numerous lavish castles, for which the French accused him of opulence. Louis XIV was genuinely interested in arts, which is mainly why he surrounded himself with some of the most prominent artists of the time – Molière, Jean-Baptiste Lully, and Charles Le Brun.

The appearance of France and the way of living has altered – the most important towns experienced a visible metamorphosis, as monuments were built everywhere, not to mention the imposing, Palace of Versailles, which remains, till today, one of the most majestic architectural masterpieces of the world. The palace improved France's prestige.

Concurrently, Louis made France self-sufficient by maximizing exports, and by carrying an economic revolution. The navy and merchant marine also experienced significant developments, and a modern police organization was established, together with ports, canals, roads – in a nutshell, the focus was directed to building an excellent infrastructure, which is a vital sign of modernity and civilization in the pre-industrial world. He embraced violent French foreign policies – he invaded the Spanish Netherlands, which he conveyed as his wife's inheritance.

However, in spite of the developments of the Reformation, Louis still perceived the adepts to Protestantism, his enemies – as he comprehended religion from a simplistic and narrow perspective. He conveyed French Protestants as rebels. Therefore, he tried to convert them by force. As he didn't succeed, he released the Edict of Nantes, which facilitated their freedom of worship in 1685. Later, he revoked the Edict, and he underwent a relentless persecution, which sent many artisans away from France.

The British Empire – the European monarchy from another perspective

The British Empire encompassed the total of colonies possessed by Great Britain. Historians argue that the British Empire achieved its peak power during the 19th century, during the reign of Queen Victoria. She became queen when she was 18, and she ruled the country for 63 years. Due to her influence as a queen, the period in which she reigned was named the Victoria era. There was a famous saying at that time – *the sun never sets on the British Empire.*

Victoria married her first cousin, in 1840, Prince Albert of Saxe-Coburg-Gotha. They had nine children, and the marriage ended tragically when he died, being 49 years old. Many years after his death, she lived in isolation, afterwards, becoming actively involved in the most important affairs of the state. The queen aimed at restoring the monarchy, and at encouraging the public to accept it, in a time in which revolts were very common in Europe. She was definitely a monarch of the people, and her involvement was factual.

During her reign, change was implemented in almost every aspect of the public life – institutional, structural, political, economic, social, and technological. Napoleon's defeat in 1815 facilitated Britain's position in shaping the European politics. Even though the **British Empire** suffered a regress, because of the American colonies, it still experienced majestic growth.

The most prominent democratic movement in Britain during her reign was enlarging the voting population when parliamentary elections took place. In 1876, and 1884, Reform Bills accomplished an increased democratization of the British politics, and at the end of the 19th century, the vote for men was universally granted. After the outbreak of the economic and industrial revolutions, the middle class in Britain experienced continual development and expansion, which resulted to an increase in business enterprising and manufacturing. Undoubtedly, industrialization played an imposing role in the urbanization process, which further facilitated the expansion of the middle classes.

Even though the reign of Queen Victoria is officially recognized as a time of prosperity, numerous challenges had to be faced. Urban poverty, accompanied by the inappropriate treatment of the working classes were problems typical of the industrialized era. Notwithstanding, in this compelling scenario, Queen Victoria was the one that promoted advancement and change, which is why, she remains, till today, one of the most prominent European figures.

Check your understanding!

1. Establish the differences between Queen Victoria and Louis IV's reign. Which were the aspects that feature their authority as monarchs?
2. Portray the way in which industrialization and urbanization occurred in the monarchial France and the British Empire.

Chapter 4 - The European Society from A Different Perspective – Two Men Who Shaped Europe's Thinking Pattern

Karl Marx

Karl Marx is widely recognized for his unusual beliefs regarding religion, as he wrote that *religion is the opium of the people*. He was one of the most distinguished sociologists, and his high-profile works, known as *The Capital* and *The Communist Manifesto,* would become one of the most representative works of the 19th century.

For starters, his work was influenced by the philosophy of George Friedrich Hegel. He stressed that ideas develop according to an endless process of contradiction, and the history of humanity is triggered by the evolution of those ideas and concepts. Hegel's philosophy had a clear impact on Marx's mentality, who was living by the idea that history is continually evolving, and the conflicts that occur lead to a predetermined direction.

Concurrently, Marx also aimed at describing the modern age, and Hegel's philosophy also influenced this characterization. Namely, even though the modern man had attained a high degree of self-awareness and personal autonomy in the 19th century, this valuable achievement resulted in the individual's alienation from the cultural and political institutions. This theme was covered, at that time in literary works as well.

Furthermore, during that period, socialism was gaining terrain among European intellectuals with radical mindsets. Although Marx felt drawn to socialism, he didn't feel satisfied with what he encountered in France, for instance, namely the Socialist Saint-Simon, who had a utopian mindset. Therefore, noticing that socialism was a naïve, idealistic movement, he decided to develop a realistic theoretical illustration of the movement, aiming at providing a deeper comprehension from a philosophic and political point of view.

Socialism as seen from a different angle

Together with Engels, Marx produced some of the most representative works of the century, such as *German Ideology* and *The Communist Manifesto,* in which, the two sociologists aimed at interpreting their ideas related to socialism, and prove the way in which socialism springs from social conflicts that originate from capitalism.

After the publishing of *The Communist Manifesto,* revolutionary agitation and unrest arose in Europe. From the abundance of works based on modern socialism, without fear of contradiction, this is the most influential and widely known. In fact, it is the syncretization of the philosophy that is known, until the present day, as Marxism. This work attempted to influence the course of history, by informing the common man about the communist movement, and what differentiates it from capitalism.

Marxism should be perceived in the context in which the work was composed. During the 19th century, the working class suffered severe hardships, in Germany, France, and England. The industrial revolution which took place during the 18th and 19th centuries established an apparent permanent underclass of workers, who lived in terrible conditions, and had no influence in the political life of the country. In fact, *The Communist Manifesto* was crafted in the context of the 1848 Revolution in Germany, featured by the utter failure of the revolution that was initiated by the working class and students.

Marx presented communism as the inevitable historical result rooted in industrialization. The working class was continually expanding, and would soon become the majority of the society. In this context, it was bound to request a change and fight against economic and political oppression, which could only be accomplished by seizing the economic and political power.

Thereupon, the European society experienced some great times: feudalism facilitated the establishment of capitalism, and in the same way, capitalism would spring the birth of communism. Marx's contribution in changing Europe was the following: he had an undying faith in the fact that communism was literally inevitable, in the course of history. Marx presented communism as the apogee of an inevitable trend in the context of the European modern world.

Marxism determined the Bolshevik revolution, which took place in 1917, and the initiation of the Soviet regime – URSS, in Russia, created a movement that was in line with Marx's concepts. This revolution affected the entire Europe, determining the spread of the movement worldwide. In the 20th century, communism was already established as a characteristic featuring the European political culture and conflict.

However, the impacts of socialism didn't stop there, and in 1945, after World War II was over, Soviet political regimes further spread in Eastern Europe. Thereupon, the most important decision of the modern time was to establish whether communism should or shouldn't be embraced. In reality, humanity's livelihood under a communist dictatorship was entirely distinct than what it claimed to be. The result being that between 1989 and 1991 communist regimes collapsed all over the world, any sense of permanence and reliability collapsed.

Sigmund Freud in the historical context

Sigmund Freud, a prevalent European personality was born in 1856. He lived through the First World War and witnessed the atrocities the war produced. In the position of an isolated neurologist, his purpose was to change the way in which society conveyed mental illnesses.

History overflows with examples of the way in which people would perceive mental illnesses. In the Middle Ages, mentally ill people were thought to be possessed by the devil, and the **Black Death** was actually considered to be the result of God's punishment over the world. People believed that the only way in which people could be cured was with severe punishment. And those who weren't willing to publicly reclaim their sins, and repent were executed publicly. Over the years, this mindset softened, and mental illnesses were considered irrational behaviors. Therefore they were often sent to institutions such as jails.

Freud was convinced that psychological causes triggered physical diseases. In this context, the development of psychoanalysis had a primary importance in the European framework since mental illnesses affected a large segment of the population. Additionally, more important is the fact that Freud developed a new pattern of thinking, pinpointing how behaviors can be interpreted – how a person's fears, wishes, and beliefs are deeply rooted in the unconscious. This hypothesis, which was derived from Freud's independent work, played a radical part in changing the way in which psychiatry is conveyed.

Check your understanding!

1. Establish the way in which the works of Karl Marx relate to the European framework of that time. In what way is his work related to modernity?
2. Highlight Freud's input in changing the thinking of the modern man.

Chapter 5: The Formation of the European Union – Putting an End to Conflict

The European Union was established in order to bring a stop to the frequent and violent disputes between European countries, which came to a head in the Second World War. Thereupon, in 1950, the European Coal and Steel Community aimed at uniting European countries, for ensuring a long lasting peace. The union initially encompassed six countries – France, Belgium, Germany, Luxembourg, the Netherlands, and Italy.

The 1950s were dominated by the Cold War between the west and east – between the countries that adopted communist regimes and the ones who rejected it. The western European nations establish the European Economic Community – EEC, also referred to as Common Market.

It is implied that the historical origins of the **European Union** lic in the Second World War. Europeans were determined to take the measurements in order to prevent the atrocities that occurred during that interval, which hindered progress.

9 May 1950

This date is officially recognized as *Europe Day*. On this particular day, Robert Schuman, French Foreign Minister introduces a plan for an extended cooperation.

18 April 1951 and 25 March 1957

In lines with the Schuman Plan, six countries agreed on running their industries of coal and steel under the same management. In this way, they couldn't have turned against one another, as it had happened at the beginning of the 20th century. Concurrently, the conflicts triggered by the Cold War, and the divisions between the east and west outlined the need for unification. On that account, on the 25th of March, 1957, the Treaty of Rome was signed, in this way; the creation of the European Economic Community was further facilitated.

1960 – 1969 – The European Union experiences economic development

Since the countries that were now part of the European Union eliminated customs duties, the European Union experienced a continuous economic growth. Concurrently, they shared control over food production, in this way making sure that issues such as famine wouldn't become problematic. In May 1968, student riots took place in Paris and many other changes that reshaped the face of Europe occurred, including embracing a more liberal mindset of life.

1970 – 1979 – The European Union is expanding

On January 1973, Ireland, the United Kingdom and Denmark proceed to joining the European Union. The regional policy takes the initiative of transferring significant amounts of money for the purpose of developing poorer European areas. The influence of the European Parliament increases, and in 1979, for the first time in history, citizens have the right to elect their members directly.

The Fall of The Berlin Wall

On the 9th of November, 1989, the Berlin Wall was pulled down, and for the very first time in 28 years, the border between West and East Germany was eliminated. Finally, Germany was reunited, and this triggered the collapse of communism all over Europe. From that moment, European politicians became more and more concerned with finding ways to ensure a better security.

The most significant question, which probably summarizes the information presented in this book, is the following: which were the primary purposes why the European Union was established?

According to the Treaty of Maastricht, which was signed on February the 7th, the European Union had the following goals:

- To sustain the democratic governing of nations
- To enhance the efficiency of participating nations
- To settle financial and economic unification
- To ensure a security policy for European countries

Since so many countries are continually adhering to the European Union, its governance implies a lot of challenges. Therefore, its structure is constantly evolving in order to become more and more efficient. Since its establishment in 1949, until today, the formation of the European Union was to foster prosperity, liberty, communication, encourage commerce and facilitate traveling. Only with continuous change and development are these aspects made possible up to the present day.

Check your understanding!

- In what ways are the factors presented in this e-book related to the formation of modern Europe? Which figures do you convey as having played the most important role in **European History**?

- Underline how embracing change is the fundamental aspect that ensured development and continual advancement.

Chapter 6 - Europe during the Colonization Era

Colonization was a reoccurring event that happened over and over again through the history of human race. However, the colonization that occurred back in late 18th century lasted until the late end of the 19th century was different than any wave of colonization before that. The first and the most important feature of this colonization wave was the development and spreading of the industrial revolution that somehow developed parallel with the colonization movement.

Unlike in some previous colonization waves back in history, this time, sugar, spice and slaves have not become the main commodity for the colonizing powers that wanted to spread their influence and power to other parts of the world. This time, industrial revolution became the central point of the colonization movement. Wanting to bring industries and technologies to other countries, industrial colonization was only yet another attempt of the major European powers to use the resource of the colonized country. Besides that, the main interest of this colonization wave became resource like cotton, wools, jute, vegetable oils and similar. However, one of the main driving forces behind the colonization in that period was how to secure enough food and resources which were lacking in Europe at that time.

The period in history between the 16th and the 20th century will go down in the world's history as a period that saw some of the most powerful colonial powers establishing colonies all over the world. During that time, European colonization powers established their colonies in different parts of the world such as Asia, Africa, South America and North America. Each big European power had its own interest sphere and acted according to that. During the initial stages of the colonial development were characterized by a policy called mercantilism that included trading that the colonial power imposed on the new colony and it implied that the colony was allowed only to trade with that colonial power. In that way, colonial forces grew their economy, but at the same time, they managed to weak their rivals which proved as a very efficient tactic. Those colonial forces included British Empire, France, Spain, and Portugal.

British Empire – the Rise and Fall

One of the most powerful empires in modern day history actually the British Empire that had colonies in almost all parts of the world. At this time distance, we can say that when British Empire was at the height of their power, they were the most powerful empire ever created on Earth. The beginnings of British Empire are actually rooted in the Portuguese and Spanish conquest. By conquering new land, Portugal and Spain established colonies that were later used as we have already mentioned for resources. Seeing what benefits brings that kind of expansionist politics, England decided to establish some of their own colonies in other parts of the world. However, England was not alone because the Netherlands and France soon followed suit and thus marked the beginning of the colonial period in Europe history.

Due to the fact that the interests of these colonial forces overlapped occasionally, many wars broke out between these colonists. At that time, British Empire has already been well established with colonies in North America and India and after the union between Scotland and England became official in 1707, Great British Empire became a force that all other colonial forces feared. However, the first blow to this once mighty Empire came in 1783 after 13 British colonies in the North America have declared independence and soon after the War of Independence, British Empire was not that fearsome anymore.

However, that would change once again in the early 19th century when British Empire was once again the most powerful empire in the world. At the moment, it possessed the strongest naval force in the entire world and because of that, that period of history is called Pax Britannica or British Peace. None of the powerful empires at that time had enough power to stand against British Royalty. Spreading from one end of the planet to the other, British Empire controlled the economy and all other aspects of the society at that time from Asia to South America.

With the turn of the 20th century, it was becoming clear that British Empire is not the only power in the world at that time. Germany and the United States have been growing very quickly, and throughout that time they obtained great economic power that challenged the British dominance and started what would later be called the final fall of the British Empire. Soon after that, World War I broke out and even though Britain did not lose any territory in that war and it even gained new territory they were no longer the dominant industrial power in the world, a title that the United States took over.

Several decades later and after another World War, the fall of British Empire was set in stone. Losing their colonies in Southeast Asia to Japan, British Empire lost one of the biggest strongholds in Asia. Even though Great Britain and the allies won in the Second World War, Great Britain can be characterized as the biggest loser of that war. Soon after the end of the World War II, India, the greatest and by far the most important colony in the British Empire gained independence, and soon after that, other colonies followed the trend, and British Empire became a shadow of his past self with features of monarchy being demoted to only ceremonial functions.

French Colonialism

French Colonial Empire was one of the greatest colonial empires in history. This Empire managed to stay alive for more than four centuries but as it usually happens with great empires they usually do not have a nice end. Similarly to the role that colonies had in British Empire, French colonies all over the world served as a resource for food, materials, and oil and France needed that badly because it had to find a way of feeding the immense army and the people back in France. In the initial phases of their colonialism, France established their first colonies in North America, Caribbean Islands and in India. Soon after that, France went to war with Great Britain and they were badly defeated in that war and as a consequence of that defeat, they lost almost all of their colonies. However, that did not stop French. Soon after that, they rebuilt the empire and this time they focused their attention on the northern part of Africa.

After the defeat in the war against Great Britain, France took some time and in 1830 proclaimed Second French colonial Empire. Even though they were defeated in the war against Great Britain, Great Britain decided to keep only four colonies that were previously ruled by France and those are Saint Lucia, Tobago, the Seychelles and Mauritius. Other colonies were returned to France. However, France did not stop there and, wanting to expand the territory and Christianity as well as French culture, France decided to conquer Algeria. However, that did not go as planned and because of that, the invasion of Algeria took more than 17 years. Besides that, France and its leader Napoleon III attempted to do the similar things with Mexico and establish a certain protectorate of colonial style in Mexico. However, that was not successful and soon after that Napoleon III and French colonial empire switches their attention to the African countries. Not only that, Napoleon III managed to put under his control a Conchin China, an area that includes parts of the southern Vietnam and Saigon. Vietnam, however, was not the only area that France with Napoleon III as a leader wanted to put under their control. Soon after establishing control over southern Vietnam, France managed to do the same in Cambodia.

During the 1870s, French efforts in Asia just increased. In that period, French established their control over Tonkin and Annam. In this period of time, France also established Indochina (a territory that included Cochinchina, Cambodia and later Laos and Kwang-Chou-Wan). In 1849, French managed to establish their control over Shanghai which only made their presence in Asia more powerful and more permanent because their control of Shanghai lasted until 1946.

With the growing influence in Asia, French colonial empire also spread in North, Central and Western Africa. During the same period of time, France managed to put under its control the following African Countries: Mauritania, Central African Republic, Senegal, Republic of Congo, Mali, Chad, Niger, Cote d'Ivoire, Benin, Guinea and in 1911 they managed to establish a French protectorate in Morocco. The final colonial efforts made by French colonial empire came after the World War I when France established control over the former Ottoman Empire territories that included today's Syria and Lebanon as well as over former German colonies Cameroon and Togo.

The fall of the French Colonial Empire began during the World War II when some of their colonies, mostly in Asia, were occupied by other powers. Japan took over Indochina, Great Britain took over Syria and Lebanon, the US and Great Britain took over Morocco and Algeria and Germany took over Tunisia. However, after the Second World War, these colonies were restored to France, but French colonial empire will not survive much longer because in almost all of their colonies a battle for independence started and it was too much for France to handle and, one by one, French colonies gained independence. One of the most problematic fights for independence occurred in Algeria because a huge number of European settlers have come during the colonization period. In 1960, a majority of French colonies were granted independence and the same happened with Algeria in 1962 after Charles de Gaulle became French Prime Minister in 1960.

Spanish Colonial Empire

The third most powerful colonial empire in Europe was the Spanish Colonial Empire. Spain was one of the first European countries to start the exploration of other parts of the world as well as one of the first countries in Europe and the world that actually started the colonization process. During the 16th and 17th century, Spanish Empire was one of the most dominant powers in the world, dominating the oceans and the battlegrounds all over Europe.

During the 18th century, Spanish Colonial Empire was the biggest in the world, with the territories and colonies in all parts of the world. However, even though 1713 saw Spain losing some of their colonies in Europe, they still maintained the control over the big American empire. Being a great and powerful player in the colonization of the America, Spain's colonization efforts reflected on the country's economy, and it saw the rise of industrialization is certain Spanish cities. Holding much of the territories in the Americas, Spain was also under constant pressures and constant wars with other great European colonization powers such as France and Great Britain.

One of the consequences of those wars was the Spanish loss of Louisiana territory in today's United States, which France took over in 1763 and soon after that France sold that territory to the United States. Spain's colonial territories in South America went through a similar process. Ruled by many years by Spanish Colonial Empire, these colonies represented a temptation and potential source of resources by other colonial powers such as Great Britain and France. Because of that and because of the fact that Great Britain has interfered and attempted to take over the colonies in South America from Spain, those colonies started their fight for independence – a process that Spanish empire that was losing power all over the world could not control or stop.

During the period between 1807 and 1821, many Spanish colonies in South America proclaimed and gained independence. Among those colonies were Uruguay, Paraguay, Argentina, Peru, Chile, Venezuela, Ecuador, Bolivia, Colombia, Mexico, Santo Domingo, Haiti. After 1821, only two colonies from the America remained a part of the Spanish colonial empire, and those colonies were Cuba and Puerto Rico. However, during 1898, Spain lost control over these two colonies as well as after the Spanish-American War. All of this was a sign that Spanish Colonial Empire is no more and that once great Spanish Empire will be just a memory.

Check your understanding!

- When did Great Britain become the most powerful colonial power in the world and which territories or colonies where part of that empire?
- What were the main reasons that European powers decided to colonize and establish their colonies in other parts of the world?
- Why did the French Colonial Empire fall and where did the beginning of that process appear?
- What motivated Spanish colonies in South America to proclaimed and to fight for the independence from Spain?

Chapter 7 - Europe during the Dark ages

The period of Dark Ages or as it is also called the period of Middle Ages is the period in European history that lasted from 5th century to the 15th century. If we are to look for one event that marked the beginning of this period that would most definitely be the fall and the dissolution of Western Roman Empire. Some of the most characteristics notions related to this period in European history are population decline, invasion, and migration. Since this period is actually representing a huge part of the European history, historians have divided it into three different periods, namely, the Early Middle Ages, High Middle Ages, and Late Middle Ages. Since each of these three periods has been characterized by different notions and events, the following part of this book will attempt to present these three time periods in the European history.

Early Middle Ages

Early Middle Ages is actually the period in European history that came immediately after the fall of the Western Roman Empire. The chaos that the fall of Western Roman Empire caused left the Europe between 5th and 8th century with many different tribes fighting for dominance. This period of European history saw Ostrogoths establishing a kingdom in Italy as well as Burgundian settling in Gaul and establishing their rule. The early middle ages also saw the Britons settling in an area what is today called Great Britain. However, these kingdoms or rule were not the only ones that appeared in the Early Middle Ages or immediately after the fall of Western Roman Empire. Other parts of Europe also saw many different kingdoms coming to power. Some of those kingdoms are the Visigoth Kingdom in what is today known as Iberian Peninsula, the Lombards kingdom in northern part of Italy, the Suebi kingdom in Iberia and several others.

Even though the Western Roman Empire was struggling for some time and eventually collapsed bringing European continent into a state of chaos, Easter Roman Empire or the Byzantine remained powerful. It has gone through a serious economic revival that made it the most dominant power in the world all the way until the beginning of the 7th century. Unlike Western Roman Empire, Eastern Roman Empire was not marked or characterized by numerous invasions and the invasions that actually occurred where the invasion of the Balkans that was at that time the western border of the Eastern Roman Empire. During the 6th century, Byzantine Empire took control over the biggest part of Italy, North Africa. Besides that, Byzantine also managed to conquer a stronghold in Spain which enabled them to have access to this part of Europe as well.

When it comes to the societies in the Western Europe during this period, it must be said that family lines of once prominent European families have died out. Besides that, other prominent families switched their attention to the matters of Church and everything that went with the Church aspect of the society. From this time distances, it seems that Western societies in that period of time wanted to get rid of all connections to the Western Roman Empire. Because of that, everything that was somehow related to the education and scholarships from the Western Roman Empire was disowned. However, one aspect of the Western Roman Empire remained important even in the period after the Empire, and that is the matter of literacy, and it had become a required skill and not only a matter of the elites. Even though cities remained the popular type of settlement after the fall of Western Roman Empire, the size and the population of those cities has decreased during the years after the fall of that Empire.

One of the consequences of the migrations and constant invasions in the period that fallowed the fall of Western Roman Empire is the disrupted trade and disrupted the economy. During the 6th and 7th century, the biggest part of Western Europe economy relied on resources from Africa. However, with the rise of Islam and Islamic Empire in the

Africa, those resources and products were not longer available for the Europeans. With no longer relying on northern part of Africa, Europe was forced to find new sources, and to a certain degree, it managed to find it in the countries in Europe that replaced the products and resources that were for so long coming from Africa. One of the most important issues that survive the Western Roman Empire was the matter of Church and Catholicism. This period also saw the beginning of monasticism in the Western part of Europe which brought Christianity even more close to the people in that part of Europe.

High Middle Ages

High Middle Ages is the period in European history that stretched over 11th, 12th and 13th century. Unlike Early Middle Ages, High Middle Ages was characterized by a sudden and rapid growth of population that appeared all over the Europe. In that regard, in around 350 years, the number of people that at that time inhabited Europe increased by more than 50 million. Even though many historians have attempted to specify the reason for such a rapid and big growth, nobody was able to precisely determine the reason. Historians are claiming that actually many factors may have contributed to this fact. Some of those factors are improved and newly invented agricultural techniques that farms used, the smaller number of slaves present in the countries of Western Europe and most importantly the lack of invasions that previously have cause deaths of a huge number of people all around the Europe.

During this period, a huge majority of European inhabitants remained rural farmers. However, unlike ever before in the history, these farms have in this period begun forming manors or what we today called villages. Besides that, the European societies at that time have been divided into sections. Those sections included townsmen, clergy, and nobility. The highest section of the society was nobility who were often called knights, and they did not own any land, but instead they used manors and the peasants for their own personal gain. This

[41]

period of history also saw the introduction of the feudalism that enabled nobility of that time to have the rights to the income that they would collect from the manors or peasants, a right granted to them by the overlord of that region. Not a long time has passed, and these rights have been considered to be hereditary.

During this period of European history, women were especially under pressure. During this period, women were required even officially required to subordinate to some male figure whether it was her husband, her father, her brother or some other male relative. Even though widows in this period were granted some freedom they were still very much limited by the male dominated nobility and clergy of that period.

This period of European history also saw the strengthening of state power. Kings and kingdoms all over Europe managed to consolidate their power and create some of the most powerful countries in the world that would last for many centuries to come. Besides the already established kingdoms such as England, France, and Spain, the High Middle Ages saw the establishment of new kingdoms that soon became very influential political powers in Europe. Some of those new kingdoms are Hungary and Poland. During this period, Germany was not displaying power that we know from history. The main reason for that was the fact that during that period Germany was ruled by Ottonian dynasty that had some serious problems in the country because they were not able to control all the duchies that comprised the Germany of that time. During this time, French monarchy also started to expand its power and its influence in other parts of the world.

The High Middle Ages were also characterized by the crusades, some of the most devastating conquest in the history of European people. During the 11th century, Pope Urban II proclaimed The First Crusades against Muslims that have been controlling Jerusalem at that time and the mission of freeing Jerusalem from the Muslim rule had become the main objective of the First Crusades. The Crusades were also characterized by the destruction of the Jewish community all over the Europe including Jewish communities in cities like Cologne, Mainz, and Worms. The destruction of the Jewish community was one of the most brutal conquests in the history of the European continent. These Crusades were not only limited to the conquest of Jerusalem or Constantinople – Crusades were also launched on the territory of Europe as well against Muslims in Spain and some other parts of the European continent.

Considering everything, High Middle Ages was a period in history that introduced some of the biggest notions that we know today such as literacy and state powers. Even though it is one of the most important periods in European history when it comes to the development of the societies, this period is also one of the most brutal periods in Europe's history mostly because of the Crusades launched for many different reasons and against many different enemies.

Late Middle Ages

Late Middle Ages is the period of European history that can be placed in the 14th and 15th century. The prosperity and the development of the High Middle Ages could not be continued in the Late Middle Ages due to many different reasons that are seen as indicators of bad times to come from this point of view and from this point in time. The Late Middle Ages was characterized by famines, which peaked with the Great Famine that appeared between 1315 and 1317. During these years, crops all over the Europe failed massively which caused a huge number of families starving, and the huge number of people died during that period. However, that was not the biggest problem of the Late Middle Ages.

In 1347, one of the worst periods of time in the history of Europe started. During that time, Black Death, a pandemic, spread all over the Europe killing a huge number of people and leaving consequences that will be felt in the coming centuries. During that pandemic, more than 35 million people lost their lives which meant that one-third of the population in the European continent has died during a very short period of time. With a smaller number of people, the economy also suffered big and agricultural manufacturers were especially hit by these events because the demand for food products reduced immensely. All of this culminated with the revolts by many different aspects of the working society throughout the entire Europe.

There was no aspect of any society in the entire Europe that was not affected by the Black Death. All these events lead to huge pieces of land being abandoned and crops failing due to the lack of working force and all of this reflected on the economy of the countries. Besides Black Death another event that characterizes Late Middle Ages is the prosecution of Jewish people from England in 1290, from France in 1306, from Spain in 1492 that eventually settled in Hungary and bigger parts in Poland.

Due to the problems with the economy and the Black Death, this period saw states increasing their power. England and France were two biggest countries that further reinstated their power based on the royal monarchy which enabled them to have huge power when it comes to the happenings in the entire Europe. However, these two states were not the only ones that saw the increase in state power. Eastern countries such as Poland and Hungary also gained immense power during this period, and in the south-western part of the Europe, a new dominant state was gaining more and more ground and that state was Portugal that will soon after become one of the most influential colonizing powers in the world.

In the end, one of the most important events that happened during this period was the fall of Easter Roman Empire or Byzantine. Weakened by many Crusades Byzantine could no longer sustained attacks from the Ottomans who eventually managed to destroy the great Eastern Roman Empire and establish one of the most powerful empires in the entire history, the Ottoman Empire. With millions of people losing their lives during this period, Late Middle Ages is characterized as one of the darkest periods in the European history.

Check your understanding!

- What were the most devastating events of the Middle Ages or as this period is popularly known as Dark Ages?
- Which countries gained power in this period and why?
- What were the consequences of Black Death in Europe?
- What were the Crusades and against who they were fought?

Chapter 8 - Europe during the Roman Empire Era

Everyone has heard of the great Roman Empire and how it shaped our old continent Europe. The Romans did not only influence Europeans, but the entire world and we even live today by the principles the Roman Empire left us as a legacy.

The Roman Empire spread on a territory that would nowadays encompass Western Europe. The Romans were holding today's Great Britain, France, Greece, Spain, the North African coast, and the Middle Est. Obviously, the most powerful European countries today once formed the unique Roman Empire, and their nations lived by the Roman Code. When we look at the EU, we can recognize a similar pattern of a unique government which means that the deeply rooted Roman origins are partially responsible for the great Union Europeans have established.

At its peak, the Roman Empire was the largest social and political body throughout Europe, i.e. western civilization in around 117 CE. The best-known man from the Roman Era is certainly Julius Caesar, the great leader, who managed to establish the great Roman Empire that is being described in history books today. He was a politician, a man of the military, and so much more.

The Rise of the Roman Empire and Caesar

Caesar was one of the most important figures in the rise of the Roman Empire, who was responsible for the shift from the Roman Republic to the Roman Empire.

Allegedly born in 100 BC of Trojan origins, Caesar became one of the greatest warriors of the Roman Empire by the age of 31. Caesar grew up in the Roman Republic which was unstable and politically disintegrated. After his military adventures, Caesar sought the company of noblemen and the powerful in order to become a part of the Roman political system. He became close with Pompey, a politician who supported the dictator Sully, after whose death, Pompey switched to the opposition. Soon, in 69 BC, Caesar was elected as a quaestor or a Roman public official. Caesar was looking for greater political influence but continued to cultivate close ties to Pompey. Caesar soon allied with Crassus, one of the leading men under dictator Sully, and one of the wealthiest men in the Roman Empire. Even if Crassus and Pompey were sworn enemies, Caesar used his great negotiation skills to appease them, and he convinced both men to join their forces which eventually gave them more power. The unity and partnership became known as the First Triumvirate in 59 BC. The main goal was to form a kind of opposition to the Roman Senate which none of the three was fond of. The alliance was quite popular among ordinary people who supported the alliance between the three. Caesar had a bigger agenda in mind, but for then, the union with the two influential men was crucial for him to establish himself as a serious political figure.

In order to gain dominance, Caesar conquered the territory of Gaul (France and Belgium). Until 50 BC he came all the way up to the Rhine River. In battle, Caesar was brutal and merciless towards his enemies and became very feared by his enemies. Even if he was away from Rome, he had his agents spying for him. The tripartite Triumvirate was shaken by internal relations, since Pompey and Crassus never really got over their disputes, and Caesar's successful battles made Pompey envious. Not long after, Crassus was killed in a battle in Syria, whereas Caesar and Pompey only deepened their disdain for each other, which led the two gentlemen to war against each other.

The war reached civil war proportions; Pompey was still backed up by the Roman nobility who considered Caesar a threat, but Caesar's military was way ahead of Pompey's, and he eventually chased out Pompey all the way to Egypt. That is where Caesar found a strong ally when he connected with the Egyptian queen Cleopatra. The war ended in Pompey's death and Caesar's return to Rome as the only dictator of Rome with a lifelong term.

Unfortunately, his lifelong term lasted only for a year when he was assassinated a year later in 44 BC. Even if in office for just a year, Caesar has introduced tremendous changes to the Roman Empire which lay the foundation for the further Roman rule. Caesar's legacy included:

- Reformation of the Roman Senate by increasing the number of Senate members,
- Local government reforms and reorganization
- Debt relief
- Carthage and Corinth reconstruction (which had been completely destroyed)
- Roman calendar reform
- Roman citizenship access to foreigners

Caesar's death was one of the most dramatic deaths in history with a conspiracy equal to Shakespeare's tragedies, when two of his Senate members, Brutus and Longinus, decided to stab him to death because they feared his ambition to become king. The Roman Senate had successfully avoided monarchical rule for five centuries by then, and they did not want the Roman Republic to become once again a kingdom.

Even if still a Republic at the time of Caesar's death, the foundations for an empire had been set since his death caused a fierce fight for power. The Roman Empire took shape when Caesar's great- grandnephew, Augustus Octavian, used his influence (based on Caesar's reputation) and military force to regain Rome in 31BC. He officially became the first Roman Emperor, and that is when the Empire was formally established.

The Roman Empire

After the official set-up, it seems that Augustus Octavian continued where Caesar has stopped. He reformed many laws, secured the borders of Rome, advocated for construction of buildings (the Pantheon among others). The time of Augustus was a time of prosperity and peace for the Roman Empire which was marked by glory and success. Octavian ruled form

31 BC to 14 CE, and he had left the Empire in marble according to his own words. After his death, the Roman Empire was on a rooky path under the leadership of his followers who lacked the vision, the will, and the power to keep Rome under a strict, but secure hand. All of the following unsuccessful rulers were known as the Julius-Claudian Dynasty since they originated from these two families.

The Roman Empire got back on track from 96 CE to 192 CE during the period known as Five Good Emperors, starting with Nerva and ending with Aurelius. This Dynasty was known as Nervan-Antonin Dynasty. Rome became strong again since the emperors expanded further in size and the political situation was also stable.

The Division of the Roman Empire

Rome was shaken up again in 235 until 284 after the rule of the Severan Dynasty (193-235) which brought Rome financial troubles due to lavish campaigns in Britain and Africa. After the assassination of the last in the Severan line, Alexander Severus in 235, Rome faced again civil warfare, battles for power and the throne which deepened the economic crisis and social uprisings. Rome ended up divided into three parts, but Diocletian reunited the Empire establishing the so-called rule of four or Tetrarchy. The order was restored to some extent, but still, the Empire had grown to enormous proportions, and Diocletian decided to separate the empire in two parts (285 CE), into the Western and Eastern Roman Empire, for easier administration and management of the empire.

After Diocletian's death in 311 CE, the empire was again stricken by warfare. The warfare was stopped by Constantine who came out the military power struggle as the winner. He gained power over both Roman Empires, and in the firm belief that Jesus Christ was his guardian in the successful battles, he initiated the Christianity campaign. He issued a series of laws on religious tolerance, especially Christianity. He advocated for written codes of faith to cherish the Divinity of Jesus with the result of collecting manuscripts which further resulted in the edition of one of the most influential books worldwide, the Bible. Constantine's reign was also marked by building the city of New Rome or Constantinople, on the territory of today's Istanbul, revaluation of the currency which was devaluated by the Severan rulers, and he also reorganized the Roman army, all of which led to the stability of the Christian Roman Empire.

After Constantine had died, the Roman unity was again in jeopardy since Constantine's sons were fighting to the death for who was going to get the larger piece. All of the three ended deadly, and the throne fell into the hands of their cousin Julian. Julian became known as the Apostate since he rejected Christianity as his faith and he made sure to remove all Christians from influential positions, banning them even from the military. He prohibited teaching and spreading of Christianity as well. After his rule, Christianity was revived more than ever with many churches that were established and different Christian centers, setting the deep roots of Christianity once for good.

The Fall of the Empire

Even if Christianity spread around rapidly, the Roman Empire had other things to deal with, like wars and attacks. The final demise of the Empire started with the invasion of Goths who significantly weakened the Empire in terms of manpower, territorial dominance, and security. The official end was declared in 476 CE when the last Roman Emperor Romulus Augustus was removed from the throne by the German king. This was the end of the Western Roman Empire, while the Eastern lasted until 1453 CE, but under the name of Byzantine Empire and it did not resemble at all the entity of the Roman Empire. It was a new empire that rested on different principles.

There were many theories about the causes that led the once great empire to succumb, and many agree that the abolishment of paganism and introduction of Christianity was one of the major reasons. But, there are also advocates who state the opposite blaming Paganism for the demise.

Nevertheless, there were many factors which contributed to the Roman Fall, and one of them is for sure the arrival of Visigoths who systematically attacked Rome until it fell apart.

The Long-Lasting Influence of The Roman Empire

Given that the Roman Empire was mostly present in Western Europe, it is quite clear why so many traditions and habits survived until today. First of all, there is the Julian calendar which was the first civilian calendar in Europe and on which the present Gregorian calendar is based. The spread of Christianity was one of the biggest successes of the Roman Empire which is visible today. Today, almost all European countries are Christian, and the Bible spread beyond the boundaries of Europe.

If we observe carefully, there are some similarities which can be drawn between the Roman Empire and the European Union. The EU is also a kind of a big empire (just in a more civil form), only with the difference that it is guided by democracy and democratic leadership. Moreover, the majority of European legislation and laws is based on the Roman laws which were well-defined keeping the Empire safe. The Roman law was very sophisticated for the time back then, and it served its purpose of keeping the Empire stable, independent, and prosperous for a very long time. The Roman Empire was also characterized by many violent uprisings, assassinations, and warfare, where every change of rule was marked by an outburst and fights for the throne. Each time a strong leader died, retreated or was killed the Roman Empire was crushed to its core with civil wars and destruction and had to be built all over again according to the vision of the new emperor. Despite the many uprisings, the Roman Empire was and remains one of the largest strongholds in the history of humanity.

Check your understanding!

- List all things that Caesar accomplished during his one-year dictatorship.

- When was the official Roman Empire established and what can be accredited to the first Roman Emperor?
- What led to the division of the Roman Empire?
- Describe the spread of Christianity, its prohibition, and revival.
- When did the Roman Empire fall and why?
- List major Roman influences that can be found in modern European society.

Chapter 9 - Europe's Influence In World Politics During the 1900's

The 1900s are a large timespan that saw the world rise and fall throughout the century. Starting with the Gregorian calendar on 1 January 1900, roots were set for the development of a modern-day and civilized society. It turned out that the world was not yet ready for a civilized approach, from bottom to top since the century was marked by European decolonization, wars and conflicts, and the rise of post-industrial revolution capitalism. All of the events contributed to the shape of Europe known today, which finally seems to have reached the highest form of civilization so far. Some of the main events are the First and Second World War, as well as the Cold War, nuclear power, exploration of space, European Union, and the beginnings of the digital age.

The New Century, Causes of the First World War and Its Outbreak

The European nations entered the new century as modern societies with a major emphasis on industrialization. The industrial revolution from the 19th century continued to grow, and people were getting used to the new powerful machinery, factories, and manufactured products. The rise of industries also enhanced the military industry, and new arms and weapons were produced making the armies very strong and powerful. It was a period when the military was heavily supported through state budgets, and the military became a symbol of prestige and success. Military strength is also one of the primary reasons that led to WWI since all the main European countries already had the necessary means and equipment when it came to one of the bloodiest events in history.

Politically, the early 1900s were a period of many political alliances were many countries signed treaties which mostly defined their loyalty to each other and granted support and assistance in case of attack. Well, these treaties led to the involvement of many countries which entered the war based on the treaties. The treaties formed the Serbo-Russian, French-Russian alliance, German-Austro-Hungarian, British-French-Belgian alliance, etc.

Even if a new century began, old habits die hard, and many countries were still looking for territorial expansion and imperialism which manifested itself in different annexations and territorial claims. This also caused a series of minor and major uprisings which were violently brought to a halt until new reign was accepted.

All of these causes led to the outburst in Sarajevo on July 14, 1914, which started WWI. That day saw the Archduke Franz Ferdinand lying dead in the Sarajevo streets when Gavrilo Princip, a Serbian radical, pulled the trigger and ended the life of the Austro-Hungarian ruler. This further led Austro-Hungary to declare war on Serbia, and in return, Russia, the Serbian allay declared war on Austro-Hungary, which finally led Germany to declare war on Russia, etc. Now it is clear how the alliances worked and what a bloody mess was created due to loyalty treaties. Not long after, almost all European countries where fighting each other, where two main alliances were set-up. We had the Entente Powers, or 'Allies' including France, Russia, Britain (the US joined in 1917) with their allies, and the Central Powers of Germany, Austro-Hungary, and Turkey with their allies. Italy was the first part of the Central Powers but switched sides in 1915 when it joined the Entente.

The First World War was brutal, claiming over 20 million lives and it ended in the defeat of Central Powers in 1981. The Peace Treaty was signed in Paris/Versailles in 1919 where the Central Powers had to accept the new armistice conditions. Germany felt especially threatened since it was stripped off a large piece of newly acquired territory and was declared the main culprit for the war. This was a huge humiliation for Germany which will seek revenge in WWII. The end of the war also led to the formation of the League of Nations, the first international organization to be devoted to maintaining peace on an international level. The Peace Conference also dismantled monarchies, i.e. Austro-Hungary, and the Ottoman Empire was also dissolved once for good. The destiny of the Balkan countries was also shaped by the conference whereby the Kingdom of the Slovenians, Serbs, and Croats was formed (which would later become Yugoslavia) including Monte Negro, Bosnia and Herzegovina, and Albania.

The new European set-up had defined clear territorial boundaries, and it was finally time to start readjusting to the new situation and the new European order and way of life. Reconstruction and restoration works started to repair the WWI damages, and Europe entered the 1920s blissfully and prosperous. A new decade had started which was also known as the Roaring Twenties.

Europe had been enjoying the fruits of its work for the following nine years until the world was hit by the Great Depression in 1929. Inflation, loss of jobs, and economic despair marked Europe until the outbreak of WW II. Only with the onset of the war, the production started to rise since new war machinery was needed and many women took over the jobs in factories since the men were in the military.

World War II

World War II remains to this day one of the greatest destructions that the world has ever witnessed. The consequences of nationalism and nationality-affiliated hatred and ruthlessness have never been clearer. With the rise of Hitler and his party in Germany in the mid-1920s, Hitler had proved to be an eloquent speaker and led the Worker's Party to the top of the government with his "patriotic" enthusiasm. Hitler was well-known for his efforts in WW I, where he served as a soldier, which could be one of the reasons why he took Germany's defeat in WW I so hard.

WW II started with the invasion of Poland by German forces and took the shape of what became known as the Blitzkrieg where the German army conquered country after country-

Netherlands, Belgium, Luxembourg, Denmark, and partially France. The war reached global levels when the USA and Japan entered the war in 1941. The casualties were enormous taking 60 million lives by the end of the war.

WW II also witnessed the first use of nuclear weapons when two bombs were dropped on Hiroshima and Nagasaki in 1945 to make Japan finally capitulate. Just after the end of the war the United Nations, as an international organization, were established. They resumed were the League of Nation stopped, but the UN was far better structured and organized with clear goals that the League of Nations lacked. Nowadays, the UN is one of the most powerful organizations advocating for peace in many conflict areas, and their influence can also be felt in other regions as well.

The Paris Peace Treaties signed in 1947 restored the borders and granted sovereignty to many states, while Germany was divided into Eastern and Western Germany. The USA and USSR, the eternal enemies, played a major role in the American and European post-war period. The world became divided by the so-called Iron Curtain which needed 40 more years to fall.

The Main Aspects of the Cold War

Even if being allies during the war, the contempt between global powers, the USA and USSR, rose tremendously in the post-war era. It was a fight for power and dominance over the global scene, and many countries were drawn into the Cold War between the two.

Europe's faith was in the hands of these two powers, whereby USA was dictating the rules for Western Germany, and USSR for Eastern Germany. Western Germany, under the guidance of America, accepted the Marshall Plan to restore its territory after the war. Eastern Europe or the Eastern Bloc was influenced by the Soviets to reject the plan, and so they did.

Europe remained torn between the two sides until the late 1980s and the beginning of 1990s. The official competition between the two began when they got involved in espionage, manufacture of nuclear weapons and engaged in the space race.

The Western Bloc adopted a new way of conduct and formed the Coal and Steel Community in 1951 which was the first document signed that led to the modern-day European Union. Italy, West Germany, Luxembourg, Netherlands, Belgium, and France signed the historical document which established a joint market for coal and steel among the Community members. This was also a way to prevent further war between these countries.

On the other hand, Eastern Germany belonged to the Eastern Bloc and its development depended on USSR, just like all other eastern countries. The Cold War was still going on, and on many occasions, it almost turned into a hot war, but thanks to the UN Treaty and many other treaties, this was successfully avoided.

The Cold War prevented Eastern Europe from a healthy social, political, and cultural development since all eastern states were subjected to the Communist regime and shared the Communist values with USSR.

One of the drastic examples of the Cold War is indeed Germany which was literally divided by the Berlin Wall, which represented the border between the two states. Eastern citizens were not allowed in and vice versa. One country was completely segregated only due to different political aspirations.

Western Europe continued to deepen its relations and ties by signing more treaties, like the Treaty on the Functioning of the European Union which was signed in Rome in 1957. Europe's policies have led to a functioning market, and the founding states started accepting new members into their treaties which made the union bigger.

Let us shift back to the Cold War which ended at the beginning of the 1990s with the fall of the Berlin Wall in 1989. This led to a complete dissolution of the Eastern Communist regime since the Soviet Union was dissolved resulting in 15 independent states. Yugoslavia, the Balkan Communist union of six countries, followed the example but the dissolution ended up in a bloodbath since Serbia violently attacked the states that tried to leave Yugoslavia. Slovenia got off the hook after three months of warfare with Serbia and embraced the Western way of life, whereas Croatia and Bosnia and Herzegovina were stuck in war from 1991/1992 to 1995. The violent war accounted for a massacre in Bosnia and Herzegovina, which is known today as the biggest massacre in modern Europe after WW II (the Srebrenica Massacre 1995).

Ironically, the European Union Treaty was signed in 1992 when the Balkan countries were already burning up in flames, as to present a unified Europe with the main focus on democracy, economic prosperity, security, and well-being. Nevertheless, Europe was united again with no western or eastern boundaries; the Iron Curtain was lifted and celebrated by a new set-up of Europe.

The European Union

The European Union was formed to establish the rule of democracy, respect of minorities, enhance economic prosperity, and cultural growth. The EU created a single internal market and the appropriate legislation which are applicable in all member states.

The initial members of the EU welcomed new members to the EU family already in the 1980s (when UK and Denmark joined) and in 1995 with the accession of Austria, Finland, and Sweden. The EU continued to grow as a strong democratic force with its own Parliament, EU Council, EU Commission, Court of Justice, Court of Auditors, and the European Central Bank.

The European Union is a unique establishment which defined Europe's way regarding all aspects, from security to justice, and as such, it became a world-recognized power which plays a major role on the global political scene. The EU managed to maintain peace and stability throughout the end of the 1990s, and it entered the new millennium with the goal to open its doors to all countries on the European territory. They are supposed to join the Union as equal members once they meet the EU criteria which include respect for democracy and minorities, adjustment of the legal system to the universal EU legislation (acquis), and economic stability to be able to compete on the internal EU market.

The Western European countries rapidly adjusted to the EU and joined it with no larger difficulties, whereas the former Eastern Bloc countries took longer to catch up with Western Europe, but many of them did by now.

Check your understanding!

- List the causes of the First World War.
- What were the major results of the Peace Treaties of 1947?
- What is the Iron Curtain? Describe the impact of the Cold World.
- The formation of the EU.
- List the main institutions of the European Union.

Chapter 10 - Europe's Influence in World Politics Today

With the conclusion of the different EU treaties which led to the final formation of the European Union in 1992 in Maastricht, the EU has grown as a strong, stable and unbreakable institution which nowadays presents one of the most important actors on the global political scene, shoulder to shoulder with the powerful USA. The EU started out with six countries, and today it counts 28 member states, and the ever-growing political body dictates the rules for many global actions and activities which require efforts on a global level.

Europe today consists of the EU member states and countries (mostly in eastern and southern Europe) which are yet to become EU members. The EU invests in these potential EU countries, guides them, negotiates with them, signs agreements and treaties to facilitate trade, border-crossing procedures, customs benefits, etc., all with the aim to have a more unified and harmonized Europe as a whole.

The EU works hard to maintain security and stability in the regions which are not yet part of the Union and offers different programs in these areas to integrate the countries as much as possible into the EU system. This means that the EU is powerful enough to set out rules for these countries in terms of political leadership, democracy, and economic development.

The EU Enlargements and Non-Member Countries

The first real EU enlargement took place in the 1970s, when the UK, one of the biggest European powers joined the Union. The UK was already invited in the 1950s to be a founding member, but it rejected the honor. After the UK joined, Denmark and Ireland immediately followed since they were closely linked to the UK (economic ties).

The following enlargement was more politically motivated than economically, when Portugal, Spain, and Greece wanted to revive democratic rule in their countries. Many other countries followed and continued to apply for membership.

The biggest EU enlargements took place in 2004 when ten East European countries joined the Union which was also a new era in the EU. The countries once belonged to the Eastern Bloc where communist roots were deeply seated, and yet they have grown to embrace democracy and the internal market.

The Czech Republic, Estonia, Hungary, Latvia, Lithuania, Poland, Slovakia, and Slovenia, andMalta and Cyprus joined in 2004, and represent the biggest EU enlargement so far. After the fall of communism, the EU tried to direct the former communist countries (not including Malta and Cyprus) towards democracy, stability, and acceptance of all values EU members share.

The Western Balkans enlargement is now priority number 1 for the EU but also for the aspiring member countries as well. The once conflict-stricken region is now consisting of candidate members and potential candidate members who are trying to meet the EU criteria. The EU dictates the criteria and provides financial assistance to the countries to help them cope with the different challenges on their EU path. One country from the Western Balkans has already succeeded in its efforts, setting an example to its neighbors. Croatia joined the Union in 2013 as the first Balkan country.

Here, we see that the EU influence is big and that many countries have to change their way of governance and life if they want to join the EU. The integration process lasts at least ten years until the countries get where the EU wants them.

What Are the Strengths of the EU?

The first thing that makes the EU influential is its economic strength. The EU is very wealthy, and as such, it has the right to be a part of major global political decisions. It has the means and the assets to dictate the course of many events like the migration crisis that hit the world after Syrian refugees fled from war-torn Syria and entered Europe. The EU took a leading role in defining the course of migration by setting up reception centers and providing shelter through special migration funds it established. Money plays a large role in the EU becoming the dominant power it is today.

On the other hand, there are 28 powerful countries which stand behind the EU and a unified decision by 28 countries has to be acknowledged on the political scene. The EU market rests on inter-linkage between the EU member states and special agreements concluded with non-EU member states. The EU market counts more than 500,000 consumers and results in stable revenues which contribute to economic stability.

The Euro

The Euro is a powerful sign of a powerful EU. It was introduced in 2002 as the official currency of the EU member states. The Euro was accepted by 19 out of 28 member states as their national currency. Many other currencies are also pegged to the Euro. Mostly, those are currencies of economically unstable countries which, in that way, are able to avoid inflation and attract investments since the euro represents a safety net. The Euro is one of the most traded currencies in the world and the second biggest reserve currency. According to Purchase Power surveys, the Eurozone ranks second as the largest economy in the world.

This also says a lot about the dominance of Europe, i.e. the EU, which has grown even stronger with the introduction of a single currency. Since the EU rests on democratic values, the EU states were not forced to take on the Euro but could keep their national currency, just like 9 EU member states did.

Has the EU Passed the USA as a Global Leader?

The EU sometimes seems stronger with its half-a-billion consumers and a stable economy than the USA who has always been the world leader in many aspects. The USA and EU have a similar annual GDP (over 18 trillion euro), but if we consider that the USA has a smaller population, then we can conclude that the USA is slightly better off. But if we consider the distribution of wealth regarding incomes, health care investments, infrastructure, education, income equality, and governance, the EU seems to have a better policy than the USA.

Still, the EU did not surpass the US unique entrepreneurial culture and technological innovations yet, while the USA cannot compete with EU as the largest manufacturer of goods and services and the biggest importer from developing countries. When it comes to the question whether it is better to be a US or EU citizen, it could be said that if you belong to the wealthy 10% in the USA, then you would be better off in the USA (since the USA is known for encouraging individualism). But, if you belong to the average population, then you could enjoy more privileges in the EU, where social responsibility is one of the key factors and where equal distribution is more straightforward than in the USA.

The European Union on the Global Stage

For many years now, the influence of the European Union has been increasing in many different aspects of the political life in the entire world. Even though it may seem that the European Union was not very much efficient on the global stage or that it does not even participate, the results show that the European Union has become one of the most important political as well as economic players on the global stage. After a certain period of time of not getting involved in the political matters on the global stage and only focusing on the economic issues of the member states, the European Union became a political union of the countries a couple of decades ago, and with that, it has entered the global political stage of the world.

Looking it from the political standpoint, there is hardly any political decision on a global stage that can be reached without the consensus from the European Union and its members. For example, over the years, the European Union has participated in creating and establishing peace treaties in many different countries all over the world. Further on, together with the United States and Russia, the European Union has become a crucial factor in reaching the agreement with Iran when it comes to the nuclear weapons and the further development of those weapons in Iran. If we take a look at the historical events, we can also see that the European Union has also been a very important factor when it comes to the matter of stopping the war in former Yugoslavia that happened during the early and mid-1990s. Ending wars, establishing peace, and helping those affected might be one of the fundamental principles on which the European Union has based its foreign policy.

Besides that, the European Union has also been one of the leaders when it comes to the climate changes. More precisely, European Union is the leading political and economic unit in the world when it comes to reducing the emission of carbon dioxide into the Earth's atmosphere. However, European Union has not stopped there. It has organized many different summits and symposiums all over the world where almost all countries in the world participated and where some very important conclusions were reached, and some very important agreement have been signed. Together with the United States and China, European Union is leading the effort of preserving our planet for the future generations.

Even though it seems that with 28 member states, it might hard to determine one and clear foreign policy, European Union has managed to do exactly that. With the one united stand, European Union has become a global player when it comes to the foreign policy as well. This has been reflected in the negotiations that each candidate state that wants to become the part of the European Union for many years now. The process of becoming a member state of European Union is not easy and quick. It demands a strong foreign policy of the candidate state and the European Union and strong negotiation abilities.

However, the biggest effect that the European Union has on the global stage is in terms of economy. With more than 500 million inhabitants, European Union is quickly becoming one of the most powerful economic forces in the entire world. Even though financial crisis has affected European Union's markets in a way that will be felt for several more years, the biggest economies in the European Union have quickly found a way to solve that problem and to end the period of crisis by becoming even more powerful economic forces. Due to its economic power, European Union has become a huge political factor in any debate on global matters in the world.

One of the biggest problems that the European Union has faced recently is Brexit or rather the Great Britain exit from the European Union. Great Britain has for many years, together with Germany, been leading factor in the European Union and Brexit has shaken up the European Union to its foundations. However, even though the consequences of that event will still be felt, European Union has managed to consolidate all 27 other member states into a unified position towards Great Britain's negotiations for leaving the European Union. The power and stability of the European Union were reflected by the ability of 27 other member states to reach a unified agreement that will be applied in the negotiations with Great Britain.

With many different challenges on the rise and with many different challenges present currently in the society of European Union, mostly the reappearance of the far right movements and the refugee crisis, European Union will be put on serious tests. European Union's foreign policy will also be put on tests because more and more areas in the world are witnessing the escalation of violence. Besides negotiations with Great Britain over the Brexit, challenges that await the

European Union in the following period revolve around terrorism, Syria, refugee crisis, the Turkey EU membership and the tremendous gain of power by far right movements all across the European Union. No matter what, the European Union has already proven to be a major factor when it comes to the politics and economy on the global stage. It has also been proven that without the European Union as a player, it will be almost impossible to reach any agreement on the global level which only serves as a proof of how important and how influential the European Union has become.

Check your understanding!

- When was the biggest EU enlargement and who joined the EU?
- The Euro and its significance.
- Compare the US and the EU market economy.
- What are some of the achievements of the European Union foreign policy?
- What are some of the future challenges that the European Union will have to face?

Conclusion

European History appears to me as an enormous book, which, even though remains open to us, seems mysterious and intricate. Many things have remained untold, and it is up to us to grasp their meaning and establish correlations.

Modern Europe is the result of the efforts of numerous people, the sacrifice of the masses, who ardently fought for a better life, change, and emancipation.

Embracing knowledge was facilitated, first and foremost, by the invention of the printing press, which also made the Reformation possible, together with the growing of the middle class. We can clearly notice how education and thirst for knowledge were the two features that characterized Europe throughout the centuries. In spite of political orientation, humankind has kept moving forward, under the reign of the monarchs, in times of capitalism, feudalism, and communism. The European Union, at the time being, plays a crucial role in the social, economic, and cultural development of the countries, as history is still being written.

I hope that this book answered the questions you had related to the history of the European continent while triggering your enthusiasm for finding out more about the subject since it's far reaching, challenging, and could never be comprised by a single work. Good luck on your quests on the historical territory!

64467003R00040